Fifi's

CRAFTY

ARTS

by Fifi Colston

ASHTON SCHOLASTIC
AUCKLAND SYDNEY NEW YORK TORONTO LONDON

First published by Ashton Scholastic, 1995

Ashton Scholastic Ltd
Private Bag 94407, Greenmount, Auckland, New Zealand.

Ashton Scholastic Pty Ltd
PO Box 579, Gosford, NSW 2250, Australia.

Scholastic Inc
555 Broadway, New York, NY 10012-3999, USA.

Scholastic Canada Ltd
123 Newkirk Road, Richmond Hill, Ontario L4C 3G5, Canada.

Scholastic Publications Ltd
7-9 Pratt Street, London, NW1 0AE, England.

© Fifi Colston, 1995
ISBN 1 86943 245 2

9 8 7 6 5 4 3 2 1   5 6 7 8 9 / 9

Edited by Penny Scown
Designed by Christine Dale
Typeset in 12/14 Gatineau
Printed in Malaysia by SRM Production Services

Contents

Hi

Ever since I can remember, I've kept busy drawing, painting and making things. As a kid, my bedroom wardrobe housed bags of essentials for craft projects; egg cartons, old magazines, scraps of material, sheepskin offcuts, used wrapping paper...
Ever the magpie, I swooped upon discarded household rubbish and transformed it into treasure.

Over the years, I've tried, tested and created crafts for a living, but mostly for the pleasure of making something from nothing much.

I like to stay away from expensive craft kits and materials: the most valuable part of a home-made project should be the idea!

To make the following ideas, you'll need the basics of glue, paint, tape and scissors. The rest of the materials you should be able to find around the house.

Invest in some concentration and good humour, and you'll have all the ingredients for successful Crafty Arts!

Cheers

Glue

A white wood or craft glue such as PVA glue is best. It doesn't smell, it isn't solvent based, and it's super strong when it's dry!

Paint

Acrylic poster paints are best. Acrylic paints dry waterproof and come in a good range of strong colours. Always wear an old shirt or apron to keep your clothes free of paint. When using spray cans, find a space outdoors — lots of newspaper and fresh air is the rule.

Tape

It's good to have a selection of tapes. Double-sided is useful for many situations where glue may be tricky to use. Masking tape is great for construction work — it's flexible and paintable.

Scissors

Use a sharp pair! Childrens' safety scissors are usually too blunt and too flimsy to use for craft work. A pair of scissors with strong metal blades and hard plastic handles are excellent for most projects. Nail scissors are useful for fiddly bits.

Craft knife

One with disposable 'snap-off' blades. Keep the cutting edge sharp — blunt knives slip easily and are dangerous to fingers in the way! When using a craft knife, put a thick piece of card or a wooden cutting board under your work.

Varnish

Try a water-based acrylic varnish. It dries quickly and cleans up with water — much easier!

Decorator Finishes

Decor Co-ordinates

Turn old objects into co-ordinating decorated items for your room. (Think carefully about your choice of paint colours and wrapping paper!)

YOU WILL NEED:

objects to decorate
3 colours of acrylic paint
gold or bronze enamel paint
attractive wrapping paper
glue
varnish
tissues

THE PAINTING:

1. Paint all over the surface you are decorating with one colour of acrylic paint. Allow to dry.

2. Pour the second colour of acrylic paint into a wide, shallow saucer or bowl. Scrunch up a tissue and dab it into the paint, wiping off any excess on the side of the dish. Dab over the painted surface.

3. Next, add a metallic look with gold or bronze enamel paint, again dabbing it on with a scrunched up tissue.

4. Finally, add a light dabbing of your third colour of acrylic paint.

THE TRIM:

5. Cut strips of attractive wrapping paper to tone or contrast with your paint effect.

6. Glue onto the painted surface as a decorative trim.

FINALLY:

7. Brush over a coat of varnish, or spray with polyurethane.

Foil Scraper Art

Inexpensive artwork that looks like a million dollars! Use it to decorate things such as matchboxes to hold small treasures, bookmarks or picture frames.

YOU WILL NEED:

> tinfoil
> glue
> thick cardboard
> methylated or white spirits
> Indian ink
> sharp knife

THE PREPARATION:

1. Glue a piece of tinfoil onto the thick cardboard. Smooth out any bumps or wrinkles with a piece of card.

2. Clean the foil surface by wiping over with methylated or white spirits, then paint the entire surface with Indian ink. Allow to dry thoroughly.

THE ART:

3. Using the tip of a sharp knife (the back of a craft knife blade is ideal), create your picture. Scrape lines into the ink with the blade, being careful not to dig into the foil.

4. When you've finished, protect your picture with varnish – acrylic varnish is good because it doesn't dissolve the ink – or you can use a light spray of hairspray.

Rag Rolling

Paint decoration with designer flair!

YOU WILL NEED:

> objects to paint
> acrylic paint (2 or more colours)
> water
> paper towels or old cotton rags

THE PREPARATION:

1. Paint your object all over with a light-coloured acrylic paint and allow to dry. This gives you a good base coat to work on.

2. Add a little water to another colour of acrylic paint and mix to the consistency of pouring cream. Pour some into a wide, shallow saucer or bowl.

THE RAG ROLLING:

3. Scrunch up a paper towel or rag (I prefer paper towels as they're easier to use and you can throw them away when you've finished — less messy!) and dip it into the paint. Wipe off the excess on the side of the dish.

4. Gently roll the towel over the surface of the object you are painting. Let dry between coats of different colours.

Découpage

This age-old way of decorating using cut-outs and varnish has been used for centuries . . . and still looks good!

YOU WILL NEED:

> object to decorate
> acrylic paints
> paintbrush
> old wrapping paper, greetings cards or magazines
> scissors
> PVA glue
> water-based acrylic varnish

THE PREPARATION:

1. Paint the tin or box you want to decorate. First brush on a plain base coat. You can experiment with layering on different coloured acrylic paints with your finger, rubbing and blending shades as you work, to produce a cloud-like effect.

2. Cut out shapes and pictures from the wrapping paper, greetings cards or magazines.

THE DÉCOUPAGE:

3. Glue the cut-outs onto the tin or box, making a montage of the pictures, e.g. a collection of flowers, or a regular pattern of shapes. Use your creativity!

4. Use the varnish to coat the object inside and out. Do about five coats (three at the very least) and let dry between coats. If you think that sounds excessive, to do découpage the real, old-fashioned way it takes up to 50 coats of varnish — and fine sandpapering after each coat! (But this looks nearly as good!)

Decorated Basket

Pretty baskets to hold jewellery, pot pourri or other treasures.

YOU WILL NEED:

cheap cane basket
light-coloured acrylic paint
Dacron filler
scissors

glue
fabric
cardboard

THE MAKING:

1. Paint the outside of the basket with diluted acrylic paint. While it's still wet, rub off the excess with a cloth. This gives a nice 'cottagey' look to the cane.

2. Cut a circle of Dacron filler to fit around the inner sides of the basket. Cut a hole out of the middle of the Dacron and slit along one side towards the centre as shown. This makes it easier to fit. Glue into place.

3. Cut a length of fabric long enough to go right around the basket and wide enough to cover a whole side and the base. Either fold 1 cm of one long edge under, or finish it with pinking shears. Glue this edge around the outside edge of the basket and let the fabric fall into the inside.

4. Cover a small square or circle of card with fabric then glue it into the centre to tidy up the lining and hide any raw edges.

5. Finally, glue on strips of fabric for decoration, as shown, then tie a bow to finish it off.

Seed Craft

Decorate a small tin with a mosaic of seeds and beans from the supermarket.

YOU WILL NEED:

> small tin or box
> black paint
> white pencil
> PVA glue
> selection of seeds, beans etc.*

THE PREPARATION:

1. Paint the box or tin black. (Matt black spray paint gives the best results.)

2. Draw a pattern onto the tin with a white pencil. Keep it simple.

LAYING THE SEEDS:

3. Pipe glue over an area to be covered with a particular type of seed. A glue bottle with a long thin nozzle (e.g. PVA glue) makes this easy.

4. Lay the seeds or beans down on the glue-covered area. It's a good idea to use tweezers to position the larger beans, while small seeds can be scattered on and the excess shaken off when the glue is dry.

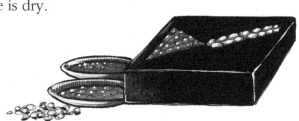

> * *Try the bulk bin section of your local supermarket. For a small outlay you can get a good selection including kidney beans, black-eyed beans, red lentils, popping corn, mung beans, haricot beans and split peas.*

Table Tidy

Graphic storage for pens, paperclips, etc.

YOU WILL NEED:

thick cardboard
scissors
cardboard tubes
glue
paint

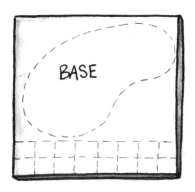

BASE

THE MAKING:

1. From a piece of thick cardboard cut out a shape about 20 cm long for the base. Also cut some small rectangles of card for decoration.

2. Trim cardboard tubes to different sizes. Shape one end of each tube with scissors.

3. Glue the flat ends of the tubes to the base, then glue the small rectangles of card around the base in a random pattern.

4. Now you can paint it! Paint the whole table tidy with one colour then add broad splashes of colour or polka dots or geometric patterns. When dry, add a top coat of varnish.

Paper Pottery

Moulded bowls from wet, mashed paper!

YOU WILL NEED:

> egg cartons
> plastic bucket
> eggbeater or potato masher
> wallpaper paste
> bowl
> plastic clingfilm
> paint
> varnish

THE PREPARATION:

1. Tear up a few egg cartons into small pieces. Put the pieces in a plastic bucket and pour enough boiling water over to cover them.

2. Every day, for about a week, mulch the paper, tearing the pieces smaller as they get softer. On the last couple of days, use an eggbeater or potato masher.

3. When the paper is really soft, squeeze out the excess water and put the pulp to one side. Mix up the wallpaper paste according to the instructions on the packet, using the water you've squeezed out. When the paste is thick and ready to use, add it a little at a time to the paper until you have a sticky pulp. Don't make it too liquid. It should be gooey like wet clay.

THE MOULDING:

4. Line a small bowl or cereal dish with clingfilm.

5. Press the paper pulp into the bowl, covering the sides and base with a thin layer. Leave the edges of the bowl uneven and ragged looking.

6. Leave to dry — about a week in the hot water cupboard is ideal. When it is dry enough to handle without crumbling, remove the papier-mâché bowl from its mould by pulling up the edges of the film and lifting out the paper bowl. Peel off the clingfilm. If the bowl is still damp, try drying it out in the oven on a low heat, or leave it in the hot water cupboard for another day.

THE PAINTING:

7. Acrylic paints are best. Paint bold patterns and designs inside and out. (Black and white looks striking when you allow the colour of the papier-mâché to show as well.) When dry, varnish to make the bowl more durable.

Face Painting

YOU WILL NEED:

a face!
face paints
sponge
paintbrush

THE PREPARATION:

1. Start with a clean, dry face. Use a headband or hairclips to pull hair back. Decide what kind of effect you want to create. It may be all over, or just a small motif like a butterfly or rose on one cheek.

2. Use a damp sponge to put a thin base coat on the face. Thin is better than thick!

THE PAINTING:

3. Squeeze your face paints into a paint tray or an old patty tin. Decide on your design and use a brush to paint the colour on. The sponge is good for blending colours on the face.

Be very careful painting around eyes! Use small amounts of paint, and light strokes of the brush, making sure you don't get paint in the eyes.

Use white paint to highlight already painted areas. For example, a bunny's nose will look more effective with a dab of white on it.

CLEANING UP:

4. Remove face paint with a warm, wet facecloth. Use makeup removal cream for any stubborn bits of paint.

Crafty Constructions

Dough Sculpture

YOU WILL NEED:

saucepan
1 cup cornflour *
2 cups baking soda *
1¼ cups cold water
paints (poster paints are best)
varnish

THE DOUGH:

1. In a saucepan, mix together the cornflour, baking soda and cold water. Cook over medium heat for about ten minutes, stirring all the time. When the mixture heats up and becomes thick, like mashed potato, remove the pan from the heat and let the mixture cool. When cool enough to handle, scrape it out of the saucepan and knead into a ball. You can use it now, or keep it in an airtight plastic bag in the fridge.

   VERY IMPORTANT: Do not add water to dough once cooked!

THE SCULPTURE:

2. Use your imagination to make interesting things from the dough. You can roll it out with a rolling pin or milk bottle then cut shapes with a knife, create texture with a fork, make holes (e.g. for beads) with a skewer or knitting needle.

   Some things you might like to make: earrings * beads * badges * napkin rings * figurines * bracelets * coasters

3. When you're happy with your creation, let it dry — the hot water cupboard is a good place. Depending on the thickness of your sculpture it may take 1-3 days to dry out properly.

4. When dry, glue on any pieces that may have come loose, then paint as desired and lastly add a coat of clear varnish.

* *You can buy big bags of cornflour and baking soda from catering supply shops.*

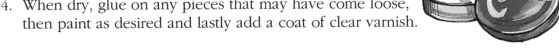

Egg Carton Orchids & Daffodils

Everlasting beauty from recycled egg cartons!

YOU WILL NEED:

egg cartons
craft knife
paint
green crepe paper
florists wire (orchid)
bendable drinking straw (daffodil)
glue or Sellotape

THE ORCHID:

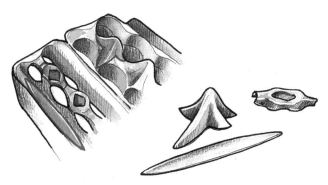

1. Cut the three shapes from an egg carton as illustrated. Make sure you trim the flower shape so that one of the points is longer than the other three. You can make five flowers and two leaves from one egg carton.

2. Take a length of florists wire and make a small loop in one end. Make a hole in the end of the flower with a darning needle or compass tip. Thread the unlooped end of the wire through the hole so that the loop is inside the flower. Thread the leaves onto the looped wire in the same way. Squirt a little glue into the flower where the loop is, then push the 'tongue' into the centre.

3. Look at pictures of orchids to get ideas on colouring then use acrylic paints to colour your orchids. Paint the leaves green. When dry, you can make the leaves curl nicely by rolling them around a thick paintbrush handle until you get a gentle curve.

4. Cut a strip of green crepe paper 1.5 cm wide. Glue the end of the crepe paper to the back of the flower just above the wire stem. Spread a little glue on the wire and wrap the stem tightly. Secure the end with glue.

   When you have wrapped the stems of the flowers and leaves, gather up the bunch and twist the stems together, then cover with a little more crepe paper to tidy it up.

THE DAFFODIL:

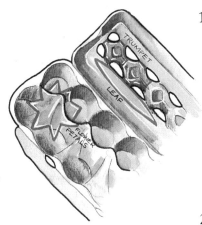

1. Cut the three shapes from an egg carton as illustrated. Cut the top third off the two trumpet pieces, paint them orange, then stick them back to back. Paint the petal piece yellow and the leaf green.

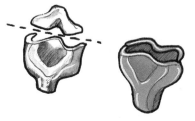

2. Wrap the straw in green crepe paper, stopping 2 cm short at the bendy end. Glue down each end. (Alternatively, use a straw, or paint one green!)

3. Push the trumpet inside the petals. Make a hole in the back of the flower, then push the straw right through it and through the trumpet, so that the unwrapped end is visible. Glue the leaf to the base of the stalk.

Memo Board

A handy reusable memo board for your room.

YOU WILL NEED:

a piece of stiff card
scissors
pictures cut from magazines or wrapping paper
glue
clear contact plastic
small piece of thin card
white-board marker pen

THE MAKING:

1. Cut a rectangle of stiff card, 20 cm x 30 cm or larger. Decorate the edges around the front of the card with magazine pictures and shapes. Glue them on.

2. Cut a piece of contact plastic 2 cm larger all around than your memo board. Peel the paper off the contact and lay the plastic sticky-side-up on a flat surface. Place your memo board face down onto the plastic, snip the corners, and fold the excess over towards the centre. Turn the board up the right way and smooth out any air bubbles.

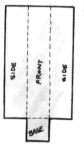

3. Cut out a small piece of card about 6 cm long and 3 cm wide with the end trimmed as illustrated. Cover it with cutouts and crease it along the fold lines indicated to form a three-sided box. Cover the box with contact plastic, allowing a 1 cm overlap at each side. Stick the box to the memo board with the overlaps, making sure the base of the box is secured with tape or contact too. This is your pen holder. Slip the pen in and your memo board is ready for action.

4. Attach it to your wall or noticeboard with drawing pins or double-sided tape.

Windowsill Kitty

A cheerful cat to sit on your windowsill, shelf or dresser.

YOU WILL NEED:

large piece of thick card
pencil
scissors
paint
strong sticky tape

5cm

THE PIECES:

1. On a large piece of thick card, copy the outline of the cat. You might like to add a little mouse, too, like I have. Also draw two small right-angled triangles and a rectangular strip slightly shorter than the length of the cat and about 5 cm wide.

2. Cut out the pieces and paint in suitable colours. (If you're not confident about your painting ability, just paint it matt black and it will make a neat silhouette!)

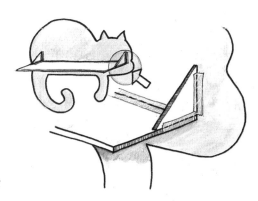

THE CONSTRUCTION:

3. Attach the small triangles to the rectangle with tape as shown. Then tape this shelf support to the back of the cat about 2 cm above the baseline of the cat shape. Sit it on your windowsill or shelf!

Balloon Masks

Decorative masks to wear or to hang on the wall.

YOU WILL NEED:

a balloon
petroleum jelly (eg Vaseline)
newspaper and tissue paper
wallpaper paste
scissors
paints

THE MAKING:

1. Blow up a balloon and tie the end securely. Rub petroleum jelly all over the balloon's surface. (This will enable you to remove the mask easily.)

2. Dip small pieces of torn newspaper into water then stick them to the balloon. Don't use any paste at this stage, but cover the whole surface with one thin layer of paper. Let it dry a little.

3. Now cover the balloon with one layer of newspaper pieces dipped in paste. Let it dry thoroughly — overnight in the hot water cupboard is ideal. Then apply another layer and dry. Do two more layers in the same way, using tissue paper for a smooth finish.

4. When the paper layers are really dry, snip the end of the balloon to let the air out. Then cut the paper balloon in half down the middle. Remove the balloon. You now have two mask bases to decorate.

THE DECORATION:

5. Cut out eyes with a pair of scissors, and trim mask to an interesting shape if you wish.

6. Paint the mask using acrylic poster paints. You might use white acrylic house paint as a base coat, which will give you a good surface on which to draw your design. If you want to wear the mask, make a hole in each side of the mask and tie on a piece of elastic.

Flax Brush

A natural garden-found paintbrush that will
cost you nothing but time.

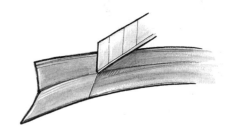

YOU WILL NEED:

> flax leaf (harakeke)
> craft knife blade

THE PREPARATION:

1. Cut a 20 cm length of flax. On the top side of
   the leaf, carefully score a light line across the
   width about 6 cm from the end. Be careful not
   to cut right through the leaf.

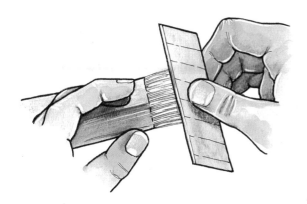

2. Holding the craft knife blade in one
   hand, and the flax leaf flat on a
   board with the other, scrape away
   the flesh of the leaf from the 6 cm
   section. Keep scraping until you
   expose the hairy fibres inside, then
   turn the leaf over and scrape the
   back until there is no green left.

3. Let the leaf dry naturally and it will
   roll up into a brush shape by itself
   over the period of a day or two,
   depending on how warm and sunny
   the spot is in which you leave it. If
   you want to speed up the process,
   you can put your brush between two
   paper towels and microwave on high
   for 30 seconds. Let it cool, and
   you're in business!

Miniature Picture Frame

Get framed in miniature!

YOU WILL NEED:

wooden curtain rings
glue
odds & ends (seeds, beans, buttons, pasta etc.)
paint
cardboard

THE MAKING:

1. Glue odds and ends onto the curtain ring to make an interesting pattern. Paint in colours to match your room.

2. Next, cut a circle of card to fit the inside of the curtain ring and glue your photo or picture onto it. The picture should sit neatly inside the ring without falling through, so make the circle of card slightly bigger than the hole in the ring. Trim the picture to fit, then apply a thin line of glue all around the edge of the picture and stick it onto the frame.

3. If you want to hang your picture on the wall, turn the screw eye at the top of the curtain hook so that it faces forwards.

If you want to sit the frame on a flat surface, unscrew the eye completely, and glue a small piece of card to the back of the picture as a prop (see illustration).

Thong Stamps

Get more mileage from an old pair of thongs!

YOU WILL NEED:

- an old thong
- craft knife
- small wood offcuts
- glue
- paper towel
- paint

THE STAMP:

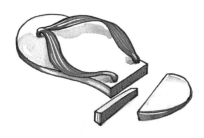

1. Cut thin slices of rubber from the thickest part of your thong with a craft knife.

2. Carefully cut out your pattern or letters from the slices of rubber.

3. Glue the rubber pieces to make the required pattern to an offcut of wood. Remember to glue your design on back-to-front (mirror image) so that it comes out the right way when you print it!

THE STAMP PAD:

4. Fold a paper towel several times and place on a saucer or plate. Dampen it with water, then put about a teaspoon of paint on it and spread it around until you have a good stamp pad.

Friendship Band

Make yourself or your friend a colourful wristband.

YOU WILL NEED:

embroidery silk (at least 4 colours)
dressmaking pins
Sellotape

THE WEAVING:

1. Cut a metre length of each coloured silk, and knot them together 6 cm from one end.

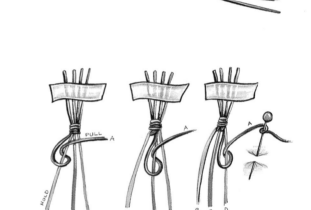

2. Sellotape the short ends onto the knee of your jeans (while you're wearing them!) and follow the instructions and diagrams shown:

    Wrap strand A over and under B to make a knot. Tighten it by holding B and pulling A up. Wrap A around C in the same way, and then around D likewise.

    To stop the band from curling up as you work, wind the strand you have just used around a pin and pin it onto your jeans.

3. Do each row of colour the same as above — always starting with the strand on the left. When the band is long enough to go around your wrist, tie the end in a knot and trim the 'tails' to 6 cm.

NB: The finished band will curl up like a snake when you unpin it — to make it flat, press it with a steam iron.

Wire Earrings

Wonderful wirey spirals!

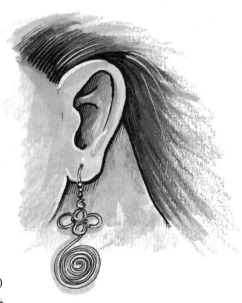

YOU WILL NEED:

florists wire
pliers (preferably rat-nosed)
newspaper
spray paint (e.g. gold poyurethane spray)
earring hooks (surgical steel — from craft
shop or jewellers)

THE MAKING:

1. Use pliers to hold the length of wire
    while you curl it and shape it into a
    spiral shape with a few loops and
    curves at the top. Make sure you
    finish with a small loop at the top to
    hang on the earring hook.

2. Put the earrings on some newspaper
    and spray with paint. Outside on a
    calm day is best. When one side is
    dry, spray the other side.

3. Finish off with the earring hooks.
    Attach to the top loop with the help
    of your pliers.

Ship in a Bottle

How is it possible?
It's all in the way you fold the rigging!

YOU WILL NEED:

> 1.5 litre plastic drink bottle
> blue play dough or Plasticine
> chopsticks (or similar)
> bamboo skewer
> balsa wood (from craft or hobby shop)
> wooden toothpicks
> paints
> scrap of fabric
> tissue paper
> thread
> florists wire

THE BOTTLE:

1. Cut the end off the bottle, leaving only a short neck.

2. Slide a sausage of blue play dough or Plasticine into the bottle. Push it into place with a chopstick, and use a skewer to flick up the surface so it looks like sea.

3. Glue the bottle onto a base of balsa wood or similar.

THE SHIP:

4. Carve a sailing ship shape, like the one illustrated, out of balsa wood. Push a toothpick and two small loops of florists wire into the bow of the ship as illustrated.

5. Make a small hole — about three millimetres deep — in the centre of the ship's deck.

6. Paint the ship with suitable colours and decorations.

THE MAST & RIGGING:

7. Make your main mast from a piece of bamboo skewer, blunt end at the top. Glue a small rectangle of fabric to the pointed end of the skewer, leaving the point free.

8. The cross pieces for the sail can be made from toothpicks. Trim one down to size for the shorter cross piece. Tie them on with thread using a one-way diagonal wrapping motion so that the toothpicks can still move freely and turn parallel to the mast. Tie long threads to the ends of the bottom spar.

9. Make sails from pieces of tissue paper, and tie on with thread as illustrated. Cut a triangle of paper to stick on the top of the mast as a flag.

10. Run the threads from the bottom spar through the two wire loops on the bow of the ship.

SETTING THE SAILS:

11. Sit the pointed end of the mast into the hole in the ship's deck. Glue the fabric to the sternward side of the deck at right angles to form a hinge. Wiggle the mast so it moves freely.

12. Fold the mast and sails down towards the stern of the ship, with the sail spars twisted so they lie parallel to the mast.

INTO THE BOTTLE:

13. Use the chopsticks to hold the ship firmly. Carefully slide it into the bottle, stern first, masts down, until you can position it on the play dough. Use a chopstick to push it firmly onto the dough.

14. Now take the sail threads and gently pull them to stand the mast up. When it is fully upright, adjust the sails with a chopstick and push the sail threads into the play dough.

Ta-da! You now have a ship in a bottle!

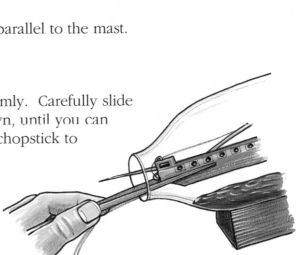

Animated Picture

Test your creativity with your own animated picture!

YOU WILL NEED:

> white paper (26 cm x 51 cm)
> pens
> thick piece of dowel, about 30 cm long
> glue or double-sided sticky tape

THE PREPARATION:

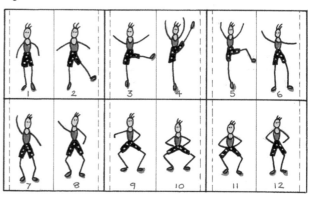

1. A sheet of A4 paper folded in half, in half and in half again will give you eight of the right sized rectangles. Rule up and label the rectangles from left to right with the numbers 1 to 12. In each box draw your animated figure. It is easiest to draw numbers 1 and 12 first, giving yourself a start and finish to work to. Then fill in the boxes in between, moving the figure or object slightly each time.

You might draw a person or an animal, a butterfly, a face or a bouncing ball. Keep it simple! Colour the pictures brightly, remembering to colour the same parts the same colour in each picture.

THE ASSEMBLY:

2. Cut between the pictures on the heavy lines, so that you end up with six sets of two drawings. Fold them in half and bend back the 1 cm overlap.

3. Glue the 1 cm flaps to the dowel, making sure your pictures follow the correct sequence.

4. Hold the dowel between your palms and roll it to and fro. Your picture will seem to move and come to life before your eyes.

Action
Attractions

Cress Heads

Eat your breakfast out of them — then grow your lunch in them!

_____

YOU WILL NEED:

an egg
sharp skewer or darning needle
nail scissors
felt-tipped pens or waterproof paints
cotton wool
Plasticine
packet of curly salad cress seeds
water

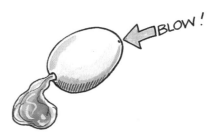

BLOW!

THE PREPARATION:

1. To 'blow' the egg, make a small hole with a skewer or darning needle at the pointed end. Make a larger hole at the other end, making sure you pierce the egg membrane. Blow hard through the small hole and the insides will come out the large one!

2. Wash out the egg well, and cut off the top third of the blunt end with nail scissors.

3. Draw a face on the egg with felt-tips or water proof paints.

THE SOWING:

4. Fill the egg with wet cotton wool. Make a small Plasticine base for the egg to sit on, and gently press the egg onto it.

5. Sprinkle a few cress seeds on the cotton wool then put the egg in a sunny place. Water it every day and watch the cress grow. After about six days, you can give it a 'haircut' — turn your cresshead into a skinhead and have a tasty addition to your salad!

Baby-Tamer

Keep a baby amused with her own personalised portable mobile!

YOU WILL NEED:

cardboard tube
black card
craft knife
Cellophane (selection of colours)
glue
corks
paints or felt-tips
coloured thread (embroidery silk or wool)
darning needle
bamboo or dowel stick

THE PARTS:

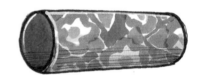

1. Decorate the cardboard tube with paints, felt-tips or brightly-coloured wrapping paper. Choose the length of your tube to suit the length of the baby's name.

2. For each letter, put two squares of card together. Draw a letter on the top piece, then use a craft knife to cut it out, cutting through both pieces of card at once.

3. Sandwich a piece of coloured Cellophane between the two pieces of card and glue in place. Repeat for all the letters. When dry, trim around the letters, leaving a black border of about 5 mm.

4. Paint or colour a cork for each letter. Put a strip of glue or double-sided tape around the middle of the cork and wind coloured thread or wool around it, a different colour for each cork. Leave a 'tail' by which to hang the cork from the mobile.

THE ASSEMBLY:

5. Punch evenly spaced holes in a line along the base of your tube (one per letter). Tie a large knot in the end of a piece of strong thread (one per hole). Poke the threads through the holes, leaving the knots inside.

6. Use a darning needle to punch a hole in the top of each letter card, and suspend from the threads at varying heights. Now make holes in the bottom of each letter and thread the tails of the corks through. Tie securely.

7. Hang the tube from one end of the bamboo stick using strong thread. Wrap brightly coloured thread or wool around the stick for decoration.

✳ *IMPORTANT: Make sure that it is always suspended out of baby's reach so that she can't suck on it or pull pieces off and put them in her mouth.*

Bean Ball

Fun, rice-filled balls to throw and catch.

YOU WILL NEED:

3 or 4 balloons (different colours)
scissors
rice

THE MAKING:

1. Cut a piece off a balloon as illustrated, about a quarter of the way along the balloon from the open end.

2. Holding the balloon open with two hands, get a friend to spoon rice into it. Push the rice down firmly and occasionally blow the balloon up a little to let the rice settle and compact.

3. Take a balloon of contrasting colour and cut a piece off the neck of this balloon, a little further along this time. Fold the end over on the rice-filled balloon so that it lies flat and stops the rice from falling out, then stretch the second balloon over it.

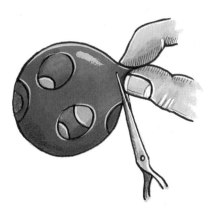

4. Repeat the process with one or two more balloons. Then, pull a bit of the top balloon away and snip it off with a small sharp pair of scissors. Do this all over, going through the next layer, too. Hey! Multi-coloured bean ball! (Make sure you don't cut through your first balloon, though!)

Robot Racer

Faster than a speeding turtle . . .

YOU WILL NEED:

empty 250 gm margarine pot
rubber band
reel of cotton (with divisions in it as pictured)
odds & ends (straws, buttons, bottletops, egg cartons, stickers etc.)
glue
paints

THE CONSTRUCTION:

1. Make three holes in the pot as shown: one in the centre of the bottom and two on opposite sides near the top of the pottle.

2. Cut through a large rubber band and thread it through the hole on one side of the pot, through the cotton reel, through the hole on

   the other side of the pot and back through the cotton reel again. Knot the ends.

Pass the end of the cotton through the hole in the bottom of the pottle and tie the end to a paperclip or small piece of card.

3. Decorate the pot. Bendy straws and bits of egg carton glued to the container and sprayed with silver paint look good. Add colour with stickers and paint.

THE ACTION:

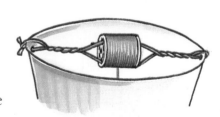

4. When you pull on the cotton, the reel twists up. When you put the robot reel-side down on a flat surface and release the tension on the cotton, the robot will skitter about.

Puffer Fish Trick

Meet Spike, the puffer fish with a noisy surprise!

YOU WILL NEED:

- cardboard box
- balloon
- paints
- cotton thread
- matchstick
- pin or needle
- small piece of thin cardboard
- Sellotape
- paperclip or wire

THE CONSTRUCTION:

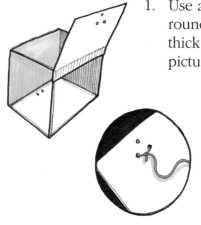

1. Use a squarish box, just big enough to hold an inflated round balloon. Make a lid for the box and hinge it with thick paper. Paint suitable puffer fish warnings and pictures on the outside.

2. Make two small holes in the bottom of the box about 7 mm apart, as shown.

3. Make three small holes in the box lid about 7 mm apart. Thread a piece of cotton through two of the holes, as shown, and tie.

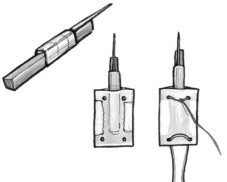

4. Tape a pin to a matchstick, then sandwich it between a piece of folded card. Tape the card closed. Make four holes in the card as shown, and tie a long piece of cotton through the top set of holes. Thread an opened paper clip or short piece of wire through the bottom set.

5. Place the pin contraption inside the box as shown and push the ends of the paper clip through the holes in the base of the box. Bend them back and tape them down out of sight beneath the box.

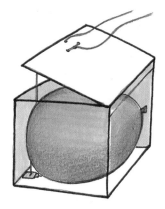

6. Blow up the balloon and put it in the box. Then carefully thread the long piece of cotton from the pin up through the hole in the top of the box. Push the lid down and tie the two threads together in a bow. Hide the bow under a sticker or small piece of card taped over it.

THE FUN BEGINS:

7. Tell someone you have a puffer fish you've raised from birth in the box, and ask if they'd like to see it.

   When they pull up the lid the thread will lift the pin up and POP!

Puffer fish surprise!

Rubbish Eater

Here's one animal that won't mess up your room!

YOU WILL NEED:

strong cardboard box
pencil
scissors or craft knife
egg cartons
2 paper cups
piece of card or paper
strip of fabric
paints
masking tape
glue

THE CONSTRUCTION:

1. Tape up the opening on the box and secure any loose flaps.

2. Draw onto the box guidelines for cutting, painting and sticking.

   X indicates where eyes, nose, feet etc. go.
   – – – – means cut along these lines.

3. Cut mouth and teeth on three sides of the box. Don't cut the back of the box — this is the hinge.

CUT OUT

4. Cut ears from the top of the egg carton.

   Cut nose and claws from the bottom of the egg carton.

Cut pieces of egg carton and thread them on a narrow strip of fabric for a tail.

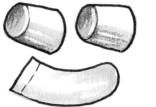

Use paper cups for eyes.

Cut a tongue from a piece of card or paper.

5. Glue all the parts to the box, except the tail. Fix this by pushing the end of the fabric through a hole in the back of the box and tying a knot inside.

6. Paint it up using a thick brush and plenty of acrylic or poster paints.

   Don't forget to feed it daily!

Paper Clip Puppets

Meet Max and Marina — dancing puppets!

YOU WILL NEED:

- paper
- felt-tipped pens
- thin card
- glue
- scissors
- darning needle or skewer
- paper fasteners
- thin wooden stick, 25 cm long
- thick cotton

THE PIECES:

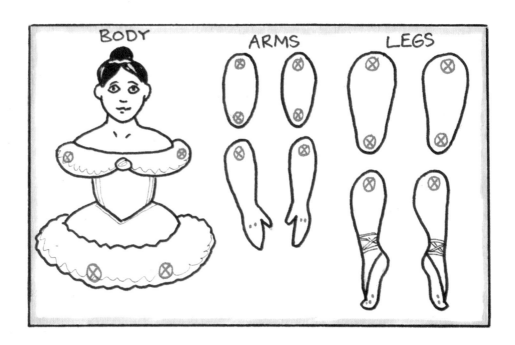

1. Trace or photocopy the puppet patterns supplied. Colour in with felt-tipped pens then glue to thin cardboard. When the glue is dry, cut out the shapes, and use a darning needle or skewer to punch holes through where indicated.

2. Use the paper fasteners to join the limbs together and attach them to the bodies. Push the fasteners through the holes and spread them apart at the back. Make sure all the joints can move freely.

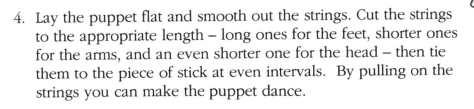

3. Thread long cotton strings through the holes marked on the hands and feet. Tie as shown.

4. Lay the puppet flat and smooth out the strings. Cut the strings to the appropriate length – long ones for the feet, shorter ones for the arms, and an even shorter one for the head – then tie them to the piece of stick at even intervals. By pulling on the strings you can make the puppet dance.

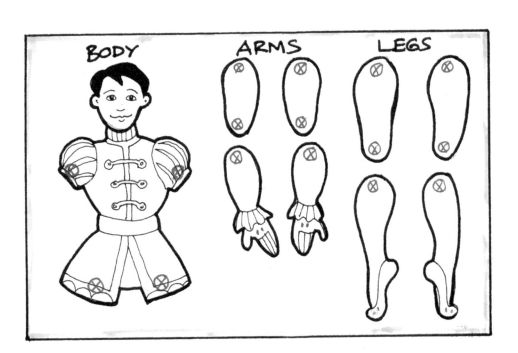

BODY   ARMS   LEGS

Drooling Alien

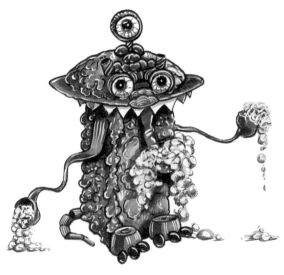

A frothing, slimy creature!

YOU WILL NEED:

odds & ends (egg & milk cartons, pie
   plates, walnut shells, pasta, buttons etc.)
glue
paints
baking soda *(not baking powder!)*
food colouring
vinegar (malt or white)

THE MAKING:

1. Build an alien creature out of junk. Perhaps a milk carton for a body, with a paper dish turned upside down for a head, pieces of egg carton for the tongue and ears, plus walnut shells for eyes, pasta shapes for nose and antennae, bendy straws for feelers and eye stalks, and dribbles of glue all over.

2. Paint it however you like!

THE ACTION:

3. Into the tongue (which must be cup-shaped), put a tea-spoon or two of baking soda. Add a couple of drops of food colouring, then pour on some vinegar, a little at a time.

Watch the chemical reaction.

Your alien will froth and drool coloured foam!

Cards & Wraps

Bubble Prints

Delicate prints for wrapping paper and cards
— from dishwashing liquid!

YOU WILL NEED:

> dishwashing liquid
> straw
> paint or food colouring
> paper
> drinking glass

THE PREPARATION:

1. Spread plenty of newspaper or a plastic tablecover over your work surface before you begin. Then, quarter-fill a glass with dishwashing liquid. Add an equal amount of water and a few drops of paint or food colouring.

2. Use a straw to blow lots of bubbles in the detergent. Keep blowing until the bubbles are high over the rim of the glass.

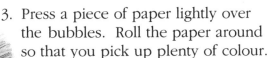

3. Press a piece of paper lightly over the bubbles. Roll the paper around so that you pick up plenty of colour.

4. Lift off the paper and pop any bubbles still clinging to it. Let it dry and you have a bubble print from which to make cards and wrapping paper.

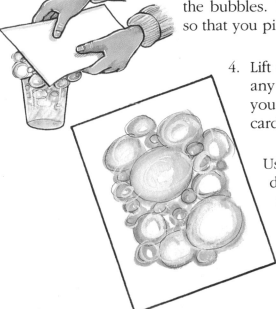

Use two, three or more glasses of bubbles, in different colours, for a really colourful print! (Let it dry between colours.)

Present Wrapper

A traditional Japanese style of gift-wrapping.

YOU WILL NEED:

> paper
> length of ribbon
> sticky tape
> a 'soft' present (e.g. scarf, socks, T-shirt)

THE METHOD:

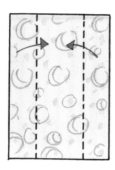

1. Start with a long rectangle of paper and mark where the folds will be. Place your folded present in the centre of the paper as illustrated, and fold the sides in to meet the middle.

2. Fold the upper corners in to meet the middle, then roll up the package loosely from the bottom end.

3. Put a piece of tape across the point – double-sided tape, or a piece of Sellotape folded into a circle, sticky side out – and finish rolling.

4. Thread a long piece of ribbon through the middle of the package and tie with a bow.

Butterfly Card

Make a three-dimensional card that looks as though it could fly away!

YOU WILL NEED:

thin card
felt-tip pens
craft knife

THE MAKING:

1. Fold a rectangle of card in half and draw a butterfly shape on the front. (Trace or copy mine if you want.) Use felt pens to make it nice and colourful. You can add some flowers to the picture too if you like.

2. Open the card out on a cutting board or piece of thick card and use a craft knife to cut around the butterfly wings – *not the body.*

3. Use your finger to bend the wings up away from the card. Voila!

Pocket Surprise

A stylish envelope for a card or present.

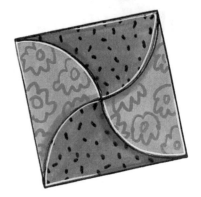

YOU WILL NEED

 2 sheets of coloured or patterned paper
 glue
 compass
 scissors
 thin card

THE POCKET:

1. Choose two colours or patterns of paper that contrast or compliment each other. Use a compass to cut out two circles 10 cm in diameter from each piece of paper (four circles in all).

2. Fold each circle in half, crease, then open out.

3. With the coloured sides face up, layer the paper circles in an alternate fashion so that the creases form a square. Glue them together where they overlap.

4. Turn over and fold down the flaps to form a pocket. The fourth flap will tuck inside the pocket to close it like an envelope.

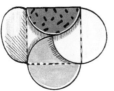 

THE MATCHING CARD:

5. If you like, you can make a matching card. Decorate a 9.5 cm square of card with scraps of the coloured paper, and write your message on it. It will slip comfortably inside your envelope.

Paper Quilling

You can make an unusual card or parcel decoration with these simple curls of paper.

YOU WILL NEED:

paper (variety of different colours)
scissors
glue (PVA or similar)
hairgrip

THE METHOD:

1. Cut your paper into strips about 5 mm wide.

2. Push one end of a strip into the hairgrip so that it is held firmly. Start twirling the hairgrip until all the paper is curled around it. Carefully slide the hairgrip out, and glue down the free end of the paper strip.

3. These are some of the shapes you can make: (a) by pinching the spiral of paper into teartrop or eye shapes as you roll it up, (b) by rolling each end of the paper separately, (c) by rolling just the very tips.

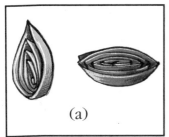
(a)

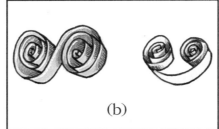
(b)

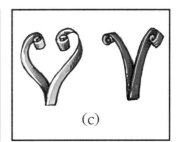
(c)

Go on, experiment! It's easy, cheap fun.

About the Author

Born in England, Fifi Colston also lived in West Africa and Scotland before coming to New Zealand and doing her schooling in Wellington.

Fifi graduated from a Visual Communications Design Course in 1980, and has spent the past 14 years as a freelance illustrator. She does all manner of artwork for advertising and children's books, and has tutored illustration as well as being a television crafts presenter on TVNZ's *What Now*. She has recently completed her own television crafts programme, *Crafty Arts*, for Kids TV.

Fifi lives in Christchurch, New Zealand, with her husband and two young children, Haley and Rory.